W9-BIC-735

Playing Through Pain

The Story of Roberto Clemente

By
Barbara Wood

Columbus, OH • Chicago, IL • Redmond, WA

The **McGraw·Hill** Companies

SRAonline.com

 SRA

Copyright © 2004 by SRA/McGraw-Hill.

Send all inquiries to:
SRA/McGraw-Hill
8787 Orion Place
Columbus, OH 43240-4027

Printed in the United States of America.

ISBN 0-07-601590-4

1 2 3 4 5 6 7 8 9 MAL 08 07 06 05 04 03

—Chapter 1—

Born to Play

Roberto Clemente always claimed that he was born to play baseball. And was he ever! As a child, Roberto played baseball every minute he could. When he didn't have a bat, he used a stick. When he didn't have a ball, he hit a tin can.

In time Roberto played on a real team. By the age of 19, he was in the big leagues. For 18 years, until his death, he played baseball for the Pittsburgh Pirates.

Roberto loved to play baseball. His fans loved to watch him because on a baseball field, he could do it all.

*He could hit to any field. He would dive for balls and catch flies. He raced around the bases at lightning speed.

But most of all, Roberto was known for his strong right arm. One radio sports announcer said that Roberto could catch the baseball in one state and throw out the runner in another state.

Fame came to Roberto late in his life. He won many awards. He became known as one of the greatest baseball players ever. He was much more than a great baseball player, however. He was also a great human being.

Roberto was proud of his roots in Puerto Rico. He welcomed young Latino players to his team. He donated his time and money to* help those from his homeland who were in need.

The daring Roberto Clemente robs New York Met
Cleon Jones of a hit. (1970)

Everyone could count on Roberto to do what was right. He said he learned this from his family. "When I was a boy, I realized what lovely persons my father and mother were. I learned the right way to live. I never heard any hate in my house, not for anybody."[1]

[1]Originally appeared in SMITHSONIAN September 1993.

4

—Chapter 2—

Baseball Kid

Roberto Walker Clemente was born on August 18, 1934. His family lived in the little town of Carolina on the island of Puerto Rico. Roberto was the youngest child in his family. He had two sisters and four brothers. Like most of the people on the island, his family spoke Spanish.

In Roberto's town, sugar was important. Almost everybody worked in the sugar business. They grew sugarcane and cut the tall stalks that are turned into sugar.

*Roberto's father, like most others, worked in the sugarcane fields. He was in charge of a crew of men who cut cane. Even though it was hard, hot work, he did not make enough money to support his family. He had to find a second job. He used an old truck to haul sand, gravel, and other goods.

Roberto's mom worked too. She ran a grocery store. People who worked in the fields bought things they needed from her store. Still, the family did not have much money.

Roberto loved his parents. They taught him to be good and kind. They taught him the importance of being honest. His parents taught him to respect adults and to help others. They* showed him the value of hard work.

When Roberto was nine years old, he asked for a bike. His dad told him he would have to earn the money to buy the bike. Roberto wondered how a young boy would find a way to earn that much money.

A neighbor was having trouble carrying milk from the store. The milk cans were heavy and hard to carry. The neighbor told Roberto that he could earn one penny a day if he delivered the milk. So Roberto carried the cans for three years.

Finally he had enough money to buy a used bike. Roberto loved that bike! He also felt great that he had learned what hard work could do.

In the winter months Roberto went to school. After school and in the summer, he helped his mom and dad with their work. Sometimes he helped load and unload his dad's truck.

Whenever Roberto had the chance, he played baseball. The weather in Puerto Rico is just right for playing year-round. Roberto played ball with his brothers and his friends. His first bat was a stick. His first glove was made from a coffee-bean sack. His first ball was a rag tied into a tight knot.

The field where the boys played was not very nice. Sometimes there were not enough children for two full teams. These things did not stop them from playing baseball. The kids played for hours. Some days Roberto even forgot to go home to eat lunch.

Roberto kept practicing. He wanted to become a better baseball player. Sometimes when he didn't have a ball, he would ask a friend to throw a tin can, and he would bat the can with a stick. He almost always hit the can.

Other times Roberto tried to build up his muscles. He squeezed a rubber ball many times. This made his arm strong.

In the evenings he lay in his bed and threw a ball against the wall. He practiced catching and throwing over and over again.

Roberto could not get enough of baseball. Sometimes he would listen to baseball games on the radio.

Other times Roberto's dad would send him to buy a lottery ticket. Roberto would ride the bus only as far as the ballpark. There he would peek in at the game. Even though he had to walk the rest of the way to the city to buy the ticket for his father, he didn't mind. He just kept dreaming of playing baseball.

At school Roberto respected his teachers. Once a teacher said that the schoolyard needed to be cleaned up. It would cost a lot of money to have this done. Roberto asked all of the boys and girls to help. They worked hard to finish the job. It did not cost the school anything.

Roberto did his best at school. His good grades made his parents happy. They hoped he would go to college. They wanted him to become an engineer. Roberto was not so sure. He was more interested in baseball than in anything else.

In high school Roberto joined the track team. He won medals for throwing the javelin. He was great at the 400-meter run. Some people thought he should try out for the Olympics. Roberto's heart was not in it. But he knew that all of the running and throwing would help him. It would make him a better baseball player.

—Chapter 3—

A Dream Come True

Roberto was batting tin cans when his first break came. The coach of a softball team watched Roberto hit can after can. The coach was so impressed he asked Roberto to try out for the softball team.

Roberto was only 14. He was younger than most of the boys at the tryouts. Still, he did very well, and he made the team! The coach gave Roberto his first uniform. It was a red-and-white T-shirt with the name of the team on it.

Roberto started out playing shortstop. Then he moved to right field. There he could make good use of his best "tool," his strong throwing arm. Whenever he made a good throw, the crowd cheered. Roberto loved it!

Soon Roberto was playing on another team. This time it was a baseball team. Roberto's baseball coach knew Roberto had talent. He kept helping Roberto play better.

One day Roberto's coach talked to a friend about Roberto. The man owned one of the best baseball clubs in Puerto Rico. This team played in the winter leagues. Many great players from the United States played with this team during the winter.

The man watched Roberto play. He said he would give Roberto $40 a week to play on his team. He also said he would pay Roberto a $400 bonus!

Roberto waits for the pitch. (1972)

14

*Roberto was too young to sign his own contract. He had to talk to his dad. Roberto's dad did not know much about baseball contracts, but he could see how much his son wanted to play. Roberto's dad thought about it and decided to sign the contract.

Roberto was very happy. He worked hard. But he sat on the bench a lot of the time. For weeks he did not play in a game. He was almost ready to quit. Then he got a chance to play. Roberto helped his team win the game. From then on, he played more and more.

One year Roberto played next to a major league star. Roberto listened to advice from the player. He* listened to other advice too. When he made a mistake, he tried not to make the same mistake again. He kept getting better and better.

Scouts from the United States came to Puerto Rico to look for new players. The Brooklyn Dodgers made Roberto an offer. They promised to pay Roberto $5,000. They would also give him a $10,000 bonus. That was a lot of money! Roberto said yes to the offer.

Soon another club made him an offer. It was for twice as much money. What could Roberto do? He had already said yes to the Dodgers, but he had not yet signed the contract.

Roberto talked to his mom. She did not need time to think about it. She said, "If you gave your word, you keep your word."[2] So Roberto signed the contract with the Dodgers.

At that time, major league teams in the United States were just beginning to include black players. The Dodgers already had four black players. Maybe this is why the Dodgers sent Roberto to play with their minor league club in Montreal. They worried about what the fans would say if they added a fifth black player. Playing in the minors was just one of the hard things Roberto had to face.

In the spring of 1954, Roberto went to Montreal to play in the minor leagues. Montreal was almost two thousand miles from Roberto's home.

Most people in Montreal spoke French. At the baseball park, people spoke English. Roberto could not speak English very well. He was lonely. Few people there spoke Spanish.

Roberto let his baseball play speak for him. Still, he had to sit on the bench much of the time. He did not understand why. When he had the chance to play, he played well.

Later Roberto learned the reason he had been sitting on the bench. The Dodgers were trying to hide him. His team did not want other teams to know how well he could play. At that time there was a rule about drafting players. Players who were not on a major league team could be drafted if they had received a bonus of more than $4,000. The Dodgers did not want that to happen to Roberto.

Soon it did happen. A Pittsburgh Pirates scout saw Roberto play. He said, "I couldn't take my eyes off him." [3] The scout said that the Pirates would draft Roberto at the end of the season. That's just what happened.

Roberto was home in Puerto Rico when he heard the news. Later he said, "I didn't even know where Pittsburgh was."[4] He was happy. He would play on a major league team. It was a dream come true.

[2,3,4] From CLEMENTE! © Kal Wagenheim. Used by permission of the author.

—Chapter 4—

Baseball Hero

Roberto played for the Pittsburgh Pirates for the next 18 years. He became a baseball hero in a city that loves baseball. "In a way, I was born twice," he said. "I was born in 1934 and again in 1955 when I came to Pittsburgh. I am thankful I can say that I lived two lives."[5]

At first, things in Pittsburgh did not go well. The Pirates lost a lot of games. They finished in last place for three years.

Things were hard for Roberto too. A reporter called him a "Puerto Rican hot dog." This made Roberto angry. Other reporters made fun of his poor English. They printed his English mistakes in the newspaper.

Roberto is tagged out sliding into home plate. (1955)

*But the fans liked the way Roberto played. They loved to watch him leap to catch the ball. They loved to see him throw the ball while he was still in the air. He did not think twice about crashing against a wall or diving into the grass to make a catch. He could bat well too.

Roberto was happy to spend hours signing autographs. He would always take time to talk to fans. Roberto's team began to get better. At the same time Roberto was playing better. By the end of his second season, he was hitting .311.

Even though his baseball career was going well, there were some other problems. While Roberto was on a trip home, a* drunk driver ran through a red light. The car crashed into Roberto's car. Roberto's back was badly hurt.

Even though the injury was painful, Roberto tried to keep playing. But he had to miss some games. Then, just when his back was better, Roberto hurt his elbow. Roberto also had painful headaches, and he had trouble sleeping. Roberto often had to play through the pain.

The 1960 season was a different story. The Pirates finished first in the National League. They went on to play in the World Series. The Pirates won!

Roberto hoped he would be named Most Valuable Player. When he did not win, it made him work even harder. He wanted to show people that a Latino from Puerto Rico could be rated with the best.

The next year Roberto played at the top of his game. He became known as a leader, and he was the team's best player. He won a batting crown for finishing the season with the highest batting average. He was also given the Gold Glove award—an award for the best fielder at each position.

Roberto returned to Puerto Rico again for the winter. One day as Roberto was mowing the grass, a rock flew up and hit his leg. Even though the pain was terrible, Roberto played in the next winter league game. But his leg injury needed treatment. After surgery he felt better. Then he got sick with malaria.

Despite more problems Roberto didn't give up. He loved being an athlete. He loved the competition, and the competition made him work harder all the time.

Roberto did work hard. He won more Gold Glove awards while playing with the Pirates. He was elected to the National League All-Star Team 12 times. In 1966 he received the honor he had wanted for so long. He was voted the National League's Most Valuable Player.

In 1971 the Pirates were again first in the National League. They went to the World Series. To win the series, a team must win four games. Each team had won three games. The last game would decide the World Series Champs!

The stadium was packed that day. Millions of people watched the last game of the World Series on television. It was the fourth inning. So far, no one had scored. Roberto was up to bat.

He hit the ball past the outfield and into the seats. It was a home run! Both teams scored another run, but the Pirates won! Roberto was named the Most Valuable Player of the World Series.

There was still one thing Roberto had not done. He did not yet have 3,000 total hits in his career. Only ten players in the history of baseball had ever done this.

On September 30, 1972, Roberto had his last hit of the season. It was the 3,000th hit of his career.

[5] From REMEMBER ROBERTO by Jim O'Brien.

—Chapter 5—

Off-Field Hero

Roberto showed that he was a great baseball player. He was also a fine person off the field.

Every winter Roberto went back to his home in Puerto Rico. In 1964 he saw one of his first teachers in a store. While they talked, a pretty young woman walked by. The teacher told Roberto that the young woman's name was Vera.

Roberto worked out a way to meet this woman. Before long he and Vera were married. They bought a house and spent the rest of the winter getting settled.

Vera and Roberto had three boys. Roberto loved his sons. Roberto loved all children. He visited children who were sick. Sometimes he helped pay for their care. Once he helped pay for a child in Nicaragua to get artificial legs. Roberto gave the child the good news in person.

In the off-season Roberto also ran baseball clinics for children. He taught children how to play. He always told them to respect their parents and to be good citizens.

At one game Roberto met a young fan in the stands. The boy was deaf. Roberto and the boy talked with their hands and their smiles. Later Roberto autographed a bat and delivered it to the boy.

Roberto and Vera with their sons before pregame
ceremonies at Three Rivers Stadium. (1970)

Roberto wanted to set a good example. He hoped winning the Most Valuable Player award would help boys and girls. "The kids have someone to look to and to follow," he said. "I show them what baseball has done for me. Maybe they will work harder and try harder."[6]

In July 1970 Pittsburgh's new stadium opened. A week later the team honored Roberto with Roberto Clemente Night. Thousands of fans came. The fans gave Roberto a giant card. More than 300,000 fans had signed it.

Roberto's wife and sons were there, and so were his parents. Roberto even helped some poor children from Puerto Rico come to the game.

Roberto used the event to help children. Fans donated more than $5,000 to a children's hospital.

*Even though it wasn't easy to be Latino in his time, Roberto was proud of his roots. When the players stopped to eat, some places would serve only whites. Only whites could stay in many of the hotels. Roberto and others spoke up. This was unfair! They did not want to be treated in this way. But these problems did not prevent Roberto from playing well.

Even when he was not playing baseball, Roberto and his family were treated unfairly. Once he and his wife went furniture shopping. The expensive furniture was on the first floor of the store. Cheaper furniture was on the upper floors.

Roberto wanted to buy some furniture on the first floor. The salesman said, "I* think we have something better for you on the sixth floor."

Roberto and Vera looked on the sixth floor. But the pieces they wanted were on the ground floor. The salesman said, "It seems to me that these prices might be a little too high for you."

The salesman thought Roberto was poor because he was Latino. Roberto knew this.

Then Roberto pulled out a stack of money and told the man who he was. Suddenly the salesman was very friendly. "Where shall I send the furniture?" he asked.

Roberto did not like the way he and his wife had been treated. "We don't want anything," he said. They walked out of the store.

Even though he was treated unfairly, Roberto treated all people well. Roberto remembered how hard it had been to be a new player from Puerto Rico. He helped young Latino players who joined the team. Sometimes he gave them money.

Roberto did not talk much about the good things he did. He just did them. He did not look for credit. He did not do things so others would notice. Often it was others who told of Roberto's good deeds.

Once, one of Roberto's friends told a story about baseball tickets. As a player, Roberto was given free tickets for his family. Many friends came from Puerto Rico to see the games, so Roberto bought extra tickets to give out. He never told anyone that all of the tickets were not free.

Another time Roberto hugged a man who was cooking food at a party. People wondered how Roberto knew the man. The man explained to everyone that he had been injured once. Roberto had helped him. The man wanted to say thanks by making all of the food for the party.

Stories such as these show what a special man Roberto was. Another baseball star said this about Roberto: "You know all about him. But in real life, he's even better."[7]

[6] From CLEMENTE! © Kal Wagenheim. Used by permission of the author.

[7] From REMEMBER ROBERTO by Jim O'Brien.

—Chapter 6—

Last Season

It was 1972 when Roberto reached 3,000 hits. No one knew it would be his last season. Roberto flew home to Puerto Rico. He wanted to rest, and he wanted to work on a plan for a new sports center to be called Sports City.

Sports City would be a place in Puerto Rico where children could learn about sports and sportsmanship. They would play baseball, tennis, soccer, and other games. There would be good coaches. The equipment would be the best. These children would not have to play baseball with tin cans and sticks.

At Sports City, children would also learn to be good citizens. They would stay away from drugs. Some children might even become famous athletes.

At the end of the year, in December, there was news of an earthquake in Nicaragua. Many people had died, and many homes had been destroyed.

Roberto had played baseball in Nicaragua. He liked the people there. He wanted to help them. Roberto put aside his plans for Sports City. He started helping with relief work for people in Nicaragua. He asked people to give food and clothes. He collected money and medicine. He helped pack boxes.

All of this work took a lot of time. Roberto worked almost around the clock. He hardly stopped to eat. He worked the day before Christmas, on Christmas Day, and the next day.

Loads of supplies were flown to Nicaragua. Soon Roberto heard that some of these supplies had not reached the people in need.

Roberto helped prepare another load of supplies. This time he would fly along. He would make sure the people received the supplies they needed.

The plane took off on New Year's Eve. But it was overloaded, and the engines were not working properly. The plane had trouble. It crashed and sank into the ocean. There were no survivors.

*New Year's Eve is usually a happy time. That year it was not. The world was in shock. Puerto Rico set aside three days to mourn their hero. The world had lost a great man.

People sent gifts of money when Roberto died. This money was used to build Sports City. Roberto's friends and family wanted to make his dream come true. They knew Roberto would want it this way. They worked hard to bring his plans to life.

Roberto was honored in many other ways. The Pirates retired the number on his uniform, number 21. A bridge in Pittsburgh was named after him. Forty schools in the United States and two hospitals in Puerto Rico also share his name.*

Roberto was the second baseball player pictured on a postage stamp. And the Roberto Clemente Award was created. This award is given to players who work hard to help people off the field.

Roberto was voted into the National Baseball Hall of Fame. This is baseball's greatest honor. This was the first time a Latino received the honor. It had been only three months since the crash. Hall of Fame rules say that a player cannot be voted into the Hall of Fame until he has been retired at least five years. The rule was set aside for Roberto.

Roberto's life was not easy. He worked hard to be a great baseball player. He worked even harder to be a great human being.

Roberto wanted to make the lives of others better. He wanted children to have more than he had when he was a child.

Today, thousands of people come to Sports City. A statue of Roberto stands at the entrance. Children play and learn on the 304 acres. Some Sports City children have gone on to become star athletes, thanks to a man some have called "The Great One."

Roberto said that if you have the chance to make the world a better place and you don't do it, you are wasting your time on Earth. Roberto lived these words each day. He wanted to make the world better, and he did.

Roberto tips his hat to the fans after his 3,000th
hit in his last game. (1972)

Roberto Clemente's

1955–72	Played for Pittsburgh Pirates
1966	National League Most Valuable Player
1971	World Series Most Valuable Player
4 times	National League Batting Champion
5 times	Led the National League in assists
12 times	Gold Glove winner
12	All-Star Games
240	Home Runs
1,305	RBIs

Career in Baseball

.317	Career Batting Average
3,000	Career Hits
1973	First Latino player inducted into the Baseball Hall of Fame (Inducted without the five-year waiting period)
1975	Inducted into the Black Athletes Hall of Fame
1984	Second baseball player to be on a U.S. postage stamp and the only one to be honored twice
No. 17	On the CNN list of the 100 best athletes of the Twentieth Century